Pakamut: Cebuano Fighting Style

G. M. Felix Roiles

Pakamut: Cebuano Fighting Style

G. M. Felix Roiles

Copyright © 2025 I&I SPORTS SUPPLY. All rights reserved. Published by I&I SPORTS SUPPLY
ISBN 978-0-934489-22-5

Cebuano Fighting Style "Pakamut"

GM Felix Roiles

First Edition

DEDICATION

This book is dedicated to my late Grandpa, Tatay Andres Roiles, my parents, Mr. Benidicto and Mrs. Francisca Roiles, to my brothers, sister, friends and relatives, people of Bonyas/Cambangkaya, Catmon, Cebu and members of PAKAMUT INTERNATIONAL ASSOCIATION, people of the Republic of the Philippines, and most of all to my children: Joseph James, Philip Gil, Francis Marben, Kenneth, Tanya Alexis, Germalane Marie, Judy Ann, Kali Marie, and Katelyn Roiles..

I LOVE YOU ALL

♥
♥
♥

ACKNOWLEDGEMENT

A special heartfelt thanks to Grand Master Dionisio Canete, founder of World Eskrima Kali Arnis Federation (WEKAF), and dean of instructional staff of DOCE PARES, Master Danny Guba and Master Val Pableo for their whole hearted support. Also a great big thanks to other instructors who I have had the chance to cross train with and who have given me inspirations. Master Jacinto Sarvida of COMBAT JUDO KARATE Federation of the Philippines (COJUKA), SGM Julius Villaflores of Philippine YAW-YAN, Master Willy Aloba Sr. of DO-KYOHAN Karate Association of the Philippines, Seifu Richard Bustillo of IMB Academy U.S.A., Punong Guro Myrlino Hufana founder of HATAI, Master Nilo Baron of PIMA SAC, Master Erwin Mosquida of LADP, Master Joe Tan of TAPADO, Master Nilo Baron of PIMA Academy Sacramento CA, Punong Guro Steven Dowd of ARNIS BALITI, GM Michael Giron of OGE, Master Oliver Garduce of Punite Martial Arts CANADA, Master Nito Noval SAC Doce Pares, Guro Roger Agbulos of LAMECO SOG, Sensei Emanuel Thomas of SANDOKAI Karate, Guro Jason Stanley of Shitorio Karate, Guro Gabe Rafael of Upakan Barabara, Master Brando Castillo, Grand Master Fred Bandalan of Bandalan DOCE PARES, Grand Master Esing Atillo of BALINTAWAK, Master Nene Gaabukayan of BALINTAWAK, Master Big John Marquez PIMA Academy, Grand Master Steve Wolk PIMA Denver CO, Guro Edwin Abo of PAKAMUT, Master Kris Paragas PAKAMUT, Toy Fernandez, Guro Ariel Moses, Guro Mike Ecdao, Master Steve del Castillo of Mt SAC Doce Pares, Master Sonny Napial of Viasayan Legacy, Guro John Garcia of Visayan Legacy, Gegie and Graham of IAM, To all the schools that supported Cebu Lion Karate Club, American Japanese Karate, KADAN Martial Art, Martial Art for Christ of Bob Mitchell. And a warm thank you to Lowel Pueblos, Master Roland and Mrs. Ferrer, Master Dong Cuesta of FIMA NJ, Lui Lendo of Canada, Fred Bandalan, Tim and Ann Ross White, Late Edgar Sulite of LAMECO, Atty. Richard Fraade, Atty. Jack Fleishli, and also to the officers and members of World Eskrima Kali Arnis Federation (WEKAF), Doce Pares Inc., and PAKAMUT INTERNATIONAL ASSOCIATION HQ. Los Angeles California, U.S.A.

Thank you all so much.

INTRODUCTION

Welcome to PAKAMUT, the origin of the Cebuano fighting style or system, or more widely known as Eskrima Kali Arnis.

Whatever your reason for deciding to study the art, whether to learn self-defense, maintain physical fitness, learn philosophy, reduce stress, develop discipline, etc., you have made the right decision.

This book is to be used as a reference source only. It is not intended to supplement or replace your instructor. This art cannot be learned from a book or manual only. Your instructor is the key to your progress in the art; without him/her you cannot learn.

The best advice that I can give you is this: Be patient. If you look ahead, this will actually slow your progress. You have to learn to crawl before you can walk.

This Art (PAKAMUT) has been a major influence and building block in my life. I hope that it will play a significant role in yours, because it has much to offer. I sincerely hope you never have to use your newfound knowledge and skills in an actual confrontation. However, if you are ever faced with imminent danger, you will have the confidence of knowing you are much better prepared to handle the situation.

CONGRATULATIONS!

GM Felix Roiles

PAKAMUT fighting system, as taught by GM Felix Roiles, was handed to him by his humble grandfather, who had much knowledge about the Filipino Fighting Art. Using a very simple method, this art utilizes the body's natural movement in highly effective forms of fighting techniques with the use of impact weapons, edge weapons and hand to hand combat.

TABLE OF CONTENTS

Page

7. Brief History of the Philippine Island

8. The Origin of the Pilipino Fighting Art

9. The Development of the Ancient Martial Art

10. The History of Pakamut

15. Solution and Formalities

17. Calisthenics

19. Proper Holding of the Weapon

22. Stance

32. Developing Physical Power

34. Classifications and Types of Ranges

88. Glossary

THE BRIEF HISTORY OF THE PHILIPPINE ISLAND

The Philippine islands lie in the Pacific Ocean off the Southeast Asian mainland, and have an area of 115,831 square miles. It is comprised of 7,110 islands, only 154 of which have an area of greater than 5 square miles. Most of the population is concentrated on 11 islands, none exceeding 1,000 square miles each, with the major area being Luzon in the north, Visayas in central and Mindanao in the south. The Population in the Philippines is approximately 98 million. The majority of the people are of Malayan ancestry. As a part of the first migration from neighboring Indonesia and Malaysia, the people in this scattered island speak 113 different dialects. Pilipino, or Tagalog, is the national language with the Cebuano leaders insisting that Cebuano language should be the national language. The main religion practiced is Roman Catholic because of the Spanish influence. 5% are Muslim, and a smaller percent consider themselves Christian. The main industry is Agriculture because of its tropical climate, but the islands are very rich in minerals such as copper, oar, and other natural resources, which are exported to United States and Japan. According to the old world of the 16th century, the Philippines is the Pearl of the Orient and Cebu is the Queen city of the south.

THE ORIGIN OF THE PILIPINO FIGHTING ART

PAKAMUT in Cebuano dialect means the 'Pilipino Fighting System and Style'. It was believed that Datu Mangal, the father of Datu Lapu-lapu, was the first Pilipino hero to bring the art of fighting to the island. Datu Mangal was a direct descendant of the leaders of the powerful Sri - Visayan Empire of ancient Malay in the 13th century, who conquered and colonized many lands. After the empire was taken over by the Maja Pahit Empire of ancient Sumatra and Borneo, the 10 datu and their kinsmen moved and settled onto the island of Visayan.

In the early 16th century, Spain expanded their territories into the Far East and landed in the Philippines. At this time, Ferdinand Magellan and his troops became the first famous foreigners to encounter the native warriors' skills in fighting. Magellan's experience of combat in the Western World was no match for the skills of the native fighters, who were trained in the native fighting style of PAKAMUT. PAKAMUT involved the use of improvised weapons such as sticks, bamboo lances and other edge and impact weapons commonly found in nature. To Spain and the Old World, Magellan was the discoverer of the new land, but to the Pilipino he was just another invader; a pirate who sought to enslave people as part of the Spanish Conquest.

On the dawn of April 27, 1521, the Siege of Mactan took place.
Ferdinand Magellan and his men invaded Mactan Island with Raja Humabon, the rival leader of the local chieftain of the main land, Cebu, and its warriors. There, Datu Lapu-lapu and his people battled Spain's finest warriors, who were armed with muskets, swords and steel body armor. But the native warriors, armed only with rattan sticks and bamboo lances, were able to drive away the invaders, leaving behind the lifeless body of their leader, Ferdinand Magellan, on the shores of Mactan Island.

After almost half a century later, the Spaniards returned with more firepower and reinforcement, and were able to gain control of the country. During the Spanish occupation of the country, its people experienced much hardship, thus beginning the 333 years in struggle. Because of the Spanish influence, the native fighting art was outlawed and the practicing of such art bas banned. Because of its unique and effective form, this art was called Eskrima Kali Arnis by the Spaniards.

THE DEVELOPMENT OF THE PILIPINO FIGHTING ART

During the time of the Spanish Occupation in the Philippines, the Filipinos still continued their training under the full moon or under the disguise of stage plays and dance. This was done until the revolutionary movements of KKK overthrew and defeated Spain in 1898. While rallying his troops during the Revolution in 1898, one of the youngest Filipino heroes, Andres Bonifacio, was noted as saying, "Go home brothers and sharpen your sticks."

When Americans occupied the Philippines from 1901 and until the Philippines was granted its independence, the Arnis became the favorite sport of royalty as a form of entertainment and show. The first martial art that was organized in 1920 was the Labangon Fencing club in Cebu Philippines. Because of the influence of the Americans in 1932, it was named DOCE PARES. Doce Pares was founded by the Twelve Masters of the Pilipino Martial Art base in Cebu, and its majority was composed of the Canete brothers, Saavedra and Venancio Ansyong Bacon. But due to some later conflicts, they split and organized their own group.

The members of Doce Pares played a major role in the resistance against the Japanese invasion in 1942. Grand Master Yoling Canete served as the President of Doce Pares from 1932 until his death in the 1980s. His son, Grand Master Dionisio Canete, was the dean of the Instructional Staff of Doce Pares and founder of the World Eskrima Kali Arnis Federation (WEKAF). Canete propagated and promoted the Pilipino Art in foreign countries. In 1979, he successfully hosted the 1st Eskrima Kali Arnis Championship in San Jose, California. Today the World Eskrima Kali Arnis Federation exisits in more than 30 countries, and stages the world championship every two years. Grand Master Dionisio Canete fielded his top instructors from all over the world to promote the art.

THE HISTORY OF PAKAMUT

The first ever documented history of the Pilipino Fighting Art, called Pakamut, pertains to the first encounter between the native warriors of Maktan Island (lead by Datu Lapu-lapu) against Ferdinand Magellan, the famous circumnavigator of the world. This encounter occurred on April 27, 1521 on the shores of the Maktan Island province of Cebu. During the encounter, the local warriors, armed only with the skills of the native fighting art along with fire hardened sticks, bamboo lances and a few steel blades, fought against Spanish warriors armed with the finest sword steel, steel body armor, cannons and muskets. Despite their well-equipped weapons, the Spanish warriors were no match for the skills of the native warriors. Few of Ferdinand Magellan's men made it back to Spain, and Magellan himself was left dead on the shores of Maktan Island.

In 1565, a half century later, the Spaniards came back again. Now lead by Miguel Lopes de Legaspi, they had more firepower and personnel, and used religion to gain control of the Filipino people. Because of the superiority of their firepower, it did not take long for the Spaniards to gain control of the islands. During those times, the practice of the art was totally banned, but became a popular form of entertainment for the Spaniards because of its gracefulness. They called it Eskrima Kali Arnis.

During the Spanish regime of more than 300 years, the Spaniards were unable to win the war against the Moros and Nitibos, who settled in the hinterlands, or mountainous, regions of the provinces. The practiced art of Pakamut was not common to the people who resided in the developed areas of the provinces, but for the locals it was part of their daily lives as a need to survive.

The art of Pakamut is categorized into 3 different styles: Long range for beginners, Medium range for intermediate, and close range for advanced. When the practitioner becomes familiar with the three category using various kinds of improvised weapons, the next segment will include the Empty Hands technique, or unarmed combat.

ATTITUDE

Firstly, what is attitude? The answer is this: It is how you perceive things in your point of view. Therefore, there is really no wrong attitude. However, there are people who have very negative attitude traits and there are those who have very positive attitude traits. We at PAKAMUT INTERNATIONAL ASSOCIATION believe that by having positive attitude, you can change and move mountains.

The first element of a good attitude is RESPECT. Respect should not only be given to your instructor and the more advanced students. You must also respect parents and elders and, most importantly, yourself. The key to understanding and respecting others is to first understand and respect yourself. At PAKAMUT INTERNATIONAL ASSOCIATION you will learn a lot about yourself.

EGO is probably the most important aspect that will govern and control your attitude. Some people will tell you they do not have an ego. This is not true, as we all have egos. What they mean is they do not have hyper-inflated egos. One should never direct his/her ego towards others in the context of comparing oneself with others. You should strive to be a better person today than you were yesterday or last week.

HUMILITY is also an important part of everyday life. Society is in turmoil today primarily because we live in generation "ME". A lot of people today have become self-centered and place themselves and their own interests above everything else. Now we can see how respect, ego and humility are connected in forming attitudes.

PATIENCE is also an integral part of your journey. The old master would not train any students until he knew them, and until they knew themselves. Today, we try to utilize shortcuts in order to accomplish most things. Fast Food and Instant Coffee, for example. Unfortunately, there are no shortcuts in learning the art of PAKAMUT. Achieving its understanding requires dedicated practice and patience.

Lastly, remember to always to keep a positive, optimistic attitude. The only real failure in life is not trying. We all have bad experiences in life, but these should not stop us from achieving our maximum potential.

PRINCIPLES OF THE PAKAMUT FIGHTING SYSTEM

Pakamut was designed by the ancient Visayan warriors to be simple to learn. The fighting system was originally used to train fellow villagers in a short period of time for combat against other island villages (tribes) and foreign invaders. There was no time or reason to teach flashy techniques or train only those with special abilities. The people had to become proficient quickly, or else perish in battle.

The fighting system is based upon natural body movements (body mechanics) that had been proven effective and could be easily taught. Datu Lapu-lapu's people depended on this fighting system's effectiveness and simplicity for their survival. This philosophy of simplicity is still used today and is the underlying base of the PAKAMUT fighting system.

THE STICK AND ITS PURPOSE

A stick is both a training tool and a weapon. The stick itself is a poor man's training tool. It trains the user in both the motions of a blade and in empty hand fighting. The strike and block motions of stick fighting translates into the blade or the knife, or into the empty hands.

The fighting system is based on the Triangle Principle. The ranges of striking are based on triangles. The far side being long range, the others being medium range and close range. The footwork, blocking, striking and empty hands are all based on triangles. The center of the body is also based on this for good fighting balance. To build a strong house you must have a good foundation. Footwork is crucial to all fighting systems. Good footwork equals good body mechanics. Good body mechanics equals a good strong foundation.

ABOUT GRAND MASTER FELIX ROILES

Grand Master Felix Roiles is a two-time World Full Contact Stick Fighting Champion, and is the recipient of numerous awards in various other martial art disciplines. Since childhood, he has spent his life in martial arts and is a descendant of Datu Lapu-lapu. He desires to teach the ancient Cebuano fighting style that he learned from his humble grandfather, Andres Roiles, who raised him in the remote mountain area of Catmon, Cebu, Philippines. At a very young age in his birth place of the mountain barangay of Catmon, Cebu, Philippines, Grand Master Felix Roiles was trained personally by his grandfather in the fighting style called PAKAMUT. In his teenage life he competed in Karate, boxing and kickboxing. He started his own group in 1983 called PAKAMUT, in honor of the art that he learned from his humble grandfather. He became affiliated with Doce Pares in 1991 and won every tournament in local and national competition in full contact stick fighting (Hosted by National Arnis Philippines (NARAPHIL)) and World Eskrima Kali Arnis Federation (WEKAF)). He then joined the Doce Pares elite team lead by Master Percival " Val " Pableo and successfully dominated the 2nd World Eskrima Kali Arnis Championship. The team defeated the rivals in 21 countries. Master Felix's Championship bout against the U.S.A. team was considered the best fight of the whole tournament, during which both fighters displayed exceptional skills. The bout resulted in a 6-time draw after the regular 3 rounds. The officials of the World Eskrima Kali Arnis Federation (WEKAF) have since amended the original rules into only a two-extension, upon which time the judges give a decision.

1994 the Philippine team again dominated the whole tournament (the United States in 2nd, and United Kingdom in 3rd), thus gaining the defending champions more popularity. In June 1996, they were given an opportunity by the Philippine Sports Commission and the City Government of Cebu to travel to the United States to participate the 3rd World Eskrima Kali Arnis Championship in California.

In 1996, after successful tournaments and demos, Felix Roiles decided to stay in the United States to promote stick fighting sports. He then opened his own studio in Carson California, participated in local community programs to promote the Filipino Martial Arts and Culture, and was given by the city of Carson a plaque of recognition for his contribution to the city. He was also awarded by the Fil-American Expo as Outstanding Community Leader in the Field of Sports on August 16, 2003 in Del Mar San Diego, California. And in December 2005 he organized the 1st Los Angeles Open Full Contact tournament in Yosemite Recreation Park Gymnasium in Eagle Rock California. It was attended by Filipino Martial Arts practitioners from all over the United States. His December 2006 2nd Annual Open Full Contact Championship (held in the same venue) was so successful that Mayor Antonio Villaragosa of Los Angeles California gave him an Award of Appreciation from the City of Los Angeles. This yearly event that Master Felix promoted drew a lot of attention from Filipino Martial Arts enthusiasts and other styles and disciplines looking to embrace the beauty of the Filipino Martial Arts. Several organizations asked him for the use of the rules he developed based in reality and by what he witnessed when he was young.

GM Felix has been featured in several news articles and papers including the May 2008 issue of Inside Kung FU magazine, International Martial Arts Magazine, FMA Digest Special Edition (an online magazine), and many more publications. He then began doing seminars for Military and Law Enforcement entities throughout United States.

"My hope is to impart the knowledge I have to people seeking the way of life of the real warrior".

Once you learn you will see the difference from before.

Weapons

Basic weapons:

        Rattan stick (scientific name)?
        That measured from 26- 32 inches depending upon the height of the person who use it, and ½ - 1" diameter. Parts of the weapon; grip area, grip area tip, shaft, long end tip.

SALUTATION AND FORMALITIES

Salutation is a sign of respect need to be rendered to show your respect to your instructor, your fellow practitioner, parents, elders and even yourself.

There are two types of salutation:
- *Formal bowing salutation.*

From natural stance, bring your left foot close to your right foot as you bring your left hand (with olisi) to the right side. Drop your left knee down to a kneeling position; raise your right hand to your forehead (palm inside) as you bow your head. Stand up and bring you left foot close to your right foot, with your left hand still holding your olisi, finally, move your left foot to the left return to normal stance.

Illustration:

- *Natural bowing salutation*

Natural bowing salutation, from natural stance, move your left foot close to your right foot, put your weapon hand in to chest and bow, then back to natural stance.

Illustration:

CALESTHENICS

Warm up: Calisthenics is very important before you start any physical activities. The way it was taught was every practitioner should warm ups to get ready of the muscles for stress strains and it starts from:

- *Neck exercise starts from natural stance with hands on the hips then rotate your neck starting from the left side then reverse, second will be the side by side neck exercise then followed by up and down neck exercise.*

- *Hands/fingers exercise, from natural stance extends both arms straight then execute by closing the hand into a fist the open.*

- *Wrist exercise, from natural stance extends both arms straight then rotate your wrist clockwise then reverse.*

- *Elbow, from natural stance extend both arms straight then bend your elbow then rotate start from clockwise the reverse to counter clockwise.*

- *Shoulder exercise, from natural stance extend both arms straight forward then rotate starting from clockwise then reverse.*

- *Body/Trunk stretching, from natural stance raise your arms on shoulder level then curve unto a 45 degree angle then move your body by looking to the left side direction then back in forth.*

- Body/Trunk side stretching, from natural stance, raise your right arm overhead and put your left hand behind your back then lean to the left side and back to the right side.

- Body/Trunk back stretching, spread your both legs apart then bend your body forward by touching the ground then come up and put your hands on the hips then lean backward.

- Hips exercise, from natural stance put your hands on your hips then rotate starting form clockwise then reverse

- Thigh stretching spread your legs apart then bend your right leg enough to touch your butt and the left leg should be straight and heal of the foot pointing up then reverse the position.

- Knee exercise, start with feet together then bend the knees and hold your knees then rotate start from clockwise the reverse.

- Ankle exercise, start from feet together then bring your body up by toes of your feet touching the ground then when you bring it down then heal up.

- Ankle exercise, from feet together lift up your right leg up about one foot from the ground then rotate starting from clockwise then reverses and then switches the left leg doing the same sequence.

FUNDAMENTALS

Holds and grip

In handling your weapon either stick or blade is very important. Your life depends upon how you handle your weapon. To make sure that you are holding it properly is to hold with your weak hand four fingers then transfer to the strong hand approximately 2 inches below grip area.

Fig. 1   Fig. 2

There are four types of holds:

- *Natural or overlapping holds.*

Illustration:

- *Side thumb*

Illustration:

- *Under thumb*

Illustration:

Reverse grip

Illustration:

STANCES

Illustration:

1. Natural fighting stance.

Illustration:

2. Back stance. (transition stance)

Illustration:

3. Cat stance (transition stance)

Illustration:

4. Hawk stance. (transition stance)

Illustration:

Form:

Practitioner will perform all the basic stances and foot works base in triangle and starts in natural stance.

1. Natural Stance

2. Feet together (closed stance)

3. Natural Fighting Stance

4. Back Stance

5. Cat Stance

6. Hawk Stance

Drills:

1. *Moving forward in natural fighting stance*
2. *Moving backward in natural fighting stance*
3. *Moving lateral in natural fighting stance (left to right)*
4. *Moving forward in back stance*
5. *Moving backward in back stance*
6. *Moving lateral in back stance (left, right)*
7. *Moving forward in cat stance*
8. *moving backward in cat stance*
9. *Moving forward in hawk stance*
10. *Moving backward in hawk stance*

Origin of the strikes
1. *Forehand slash (high, med and low line target)*

2. *Backhand slash (high, med and low line target)*

FOREHAND STRIKES

BACK HAND STRIKES

Forms:
1. *Forehand and backhand slash downward (high line)*
2. *Forehand and backhand slash downward (med sec)*
3. *Forehand and backhand slash downward (low line target ei, legs)*
4. *Forehand and backhand slash upward (also known as figure 8)*
5. *Palm down trust (strike comes from right hand side)*
6. *Palm up trust (strike comes from the opposite side)*

Drills
1. Moving forward in natural fighting stance plus forehand and backhand slash strike.
2. Moving backward in natural fighting stance plus forehand and backhand slash strike
3. Moving lateral (left to right, right to left) in natural fighting stance with forehand and backhand slash strikes
4. Moving forward in back stance plus forehand and backhand slash strike
5. Moving backward in back stance plus forehand and backhand slash strike
6. Moving lateral (left to right, right to left) in back fighting stance with forehand and backhand slash strikes.
7. Moving forward in cat stance plus forehand and backhand slash strike
8. moving backward in cat stance plus forehand and backhand slash strike
9. Moving forward in hawk stance plus forehand and backhand slash strike
10. Moving backward in hawk stance plus forehand and backhand slash strike.

Basic blocking Technique

1. Vertical (upward and downward position)
   Vertical upward position

Downward position

2. Diagonal (downward and upward position)

Blocking

The ability to block is as important as the ability to hit! Anybody can hit but not everybody can block because they are not trained to. Learn to block quickly and counter strike. First learn to get in the ready position quickly. Stick in the right hand at angle to make one side of the angle. Left hand (checking hand) ready to check at an angle this makes the other side of the angle. Your palm edge should be against the stick so you do not get struck by the recoil of your opponent's strike. Your hip's being squared up makes the third. Your stick should never be further than the width of your hand spread away from your body. This allows you to have efficiency in motion a critical concept.

Blocking is the ability to intercept your opponents strike to avoid of getting hit with the weapon. To do this properly you need to have a lot of leverage proper footwork and not extending your arm to far from your body and should use the weak hand as a secondary block.

Technique 1: Natural stance-move your weapon to left and right side of the area that you intended to protect and followed by your weak hand as a secondary block. The weapon should be kept about 6 inches from the body or even closer to have more leverage.

Form 1: From natural stance, slide your lead foot forward to fighting forward stance and block the incoming strike either a diagonal or vertical block, using your weapon and support with your weak hand.

Form 2: From natural stance, slide your weak side foot backward to fighting forward stance and block the incoming strike either a diagonal or vertical block, using your weapon and support with your weak hand.

Form 3: From natural stance, slide your back foot to the side about 6 inches as the lead foot follow in to a fighting forward stance (lateral left) and block the incoming strike either a diagonal or vertical block, using your weapon and support with your weak hand.

Form 4: From natural stance, slide your lead foot to the side about 6 inches to the side as the back foot follow into a lateral move to the right side fighting forward stance and block the incoming strike either a diagonal or vertical block, using your weapon and support with your weak hand.

Drill 1: From natural stance, slide your lead foot forward and block the incoming strike either a diagonal or vertical block using your weapon and support with your weak hand then counter with a backhand strike.

Drill 2: From natural stance, slide your lead foot forward and block the incoming strike either a diagonal or vertical block using your weapon and support with your weak hand then counter with a backhand strike then block the next strike.

Drill 3: From natural stance, slide your lead foot forward and block the incoming strike either a diagonal or vertical block using your weapon and support with your weak hand then counter with a backhand strike then block the next strike.

Drill 4: From natural stance, slide your lead foot forward and block the incoming strike either a diagonal or vertical block using your weapon and support with your weak hand then counter with a backhand strike then block the next strike.

DEVELOPING PHYSICAL POWERS

The two central tenets of physical power in FMA (Filipino Martial Art) are relaxation and total body commitment to the blow. Relaxation and physical looseness is often a surprise to a new practitioner of FMA training; generally, a tensed muscle is associated with strength. However, a tense muscle is a slow muscle, and blows have to be delivered with speed otherwise they can simply become forceful pushes rather than debilitating strikes. Any successful FMA technique should use a mixture of relaxation and tension. In the case of a strike for instance, the arm should be kept as loose as possible prior to actual contact with the target, thus allowing the stick to whip out with speed. Tension is, however, required upon actual contact, locking every muscle in the body to provide a solid base for the transference of energy from the strike into the target. This locking of the body in turn indicates the essential principle of total body commitment. Using the split-second locking of the body on impact and an absolute commitment of the whole frame to any blow strike, anyone can generate enormous destructive impact. Particularly vital is control of the waist and the shoulder as these points, if not properly solid, can twist on impact and retract some of the force. The moment of contact can be accompanied by a shout. This is not just for intimidation, shouting forces air from the body and this greatly increases muscle tension in the chest and abdomen for more solid attacks.

CLASIFICATION and method of fighting

1. Long range fighting, is the style of fighting which you can reach your opponent weapon hand with your weapon and your opponent can do the same. The focus target will be the weapon hand and these techniques will be the first stage of the beginners as a process of learning and understanding the concept of the Filipino Fighting Art.

2. Medium range fighting, is a method of fighting which you can reach your opponents torso and other parts of the body by your weapon and your opponent can do the same, this also consider as the second phase of training, which employ various strikes angles foot works distance, multiple counter strikes, breaking, takedowns, throws locks and submission.

3. Close range fighting, is the method of fighting which you will be able to reach your opponent face with your bare hand, which employ various strikes angles foot works distance, multiple counter strikes, breaking, takedowns, throws locks and submission.

LAGYO (Long range)

Striking Patterns for Long Range Single Stick Fighting

The long range basic striking pattern is based on a 6 strike angles. The six strikes is easy pattern to remember. The saying is that you must de-fang the snake first! This covers the first two strikes. If it can not move it can not strike. This covers the second two. If it can not breathe it cannot fight! This explains the last two.

Basic Long Range Strike # 1- 1.Thecnique: Downward strike across the weapon hand. This can be done to either the right or left hand. 2. Form: Assume fighting forward stance with the weapon in on guard position. 3. Drill: From natural stance, slide your lead foot to the front and deliver a forehand slash cross the body or the weapon hand defending on your distance or ranges.

Basic Long Range Strike #2 - 1. Technique: Upward across the weapon hand. This can be done to either the right or left hand.
2. Form: Assume fighting forward stance with the weapon in on guard position.
3. Drill: From natural stance, slide your lead foot to the front and deliver a forehand slash cross the body or the weapon hand defending on your distance or ranges.

Basic Long Range Strike #3 - 1. Technique: Upward across the body from the right hip to the left shoulder-collar bone.
2. Form: Assume fighting forward stance with the weapon in on guard position.
3. Drill: From natural stance, slide your lead foot to the front and deliver an upward forehand slash cross the body or the weapon hand defending on your distance or ranges.

Basic Long Range Strike #4- 1. Technique: Downward across the body from left shoulder collar bone to the right hip.
2. Form: Assume fighting forward stance with the weapon in on guard position.
3. Drill: From natural stance, slide your lead foot to the front and deliver a forehand slash cross the body or the weapon hand defending on your distance or ranges.

Basic Long Range Strike #5- 1. Technique: Forehand slash across the med section of the body.

2. Form: From natural stance, assume fighting forward stance with the weapon in on guard position.

3. Drill: From natural stance, slide your lead foot to the front and deliver a forehand horizontal forehand slash cross the body or the weapon hand defending on your distance or ranges.

Basic Long Range Strike #6- 1. Technique: Backhand slash across the med section of the body.

2. Form: From natural stance, assume fighting forward stance with the weapon in on guard position.

3. Drill: From natural stance, slide your lead foot to the front and deliver a forehand slash cross the body or the weapon hand defending on your distance or ranges.

Illustration:

Strike one

Strike two

Strike three

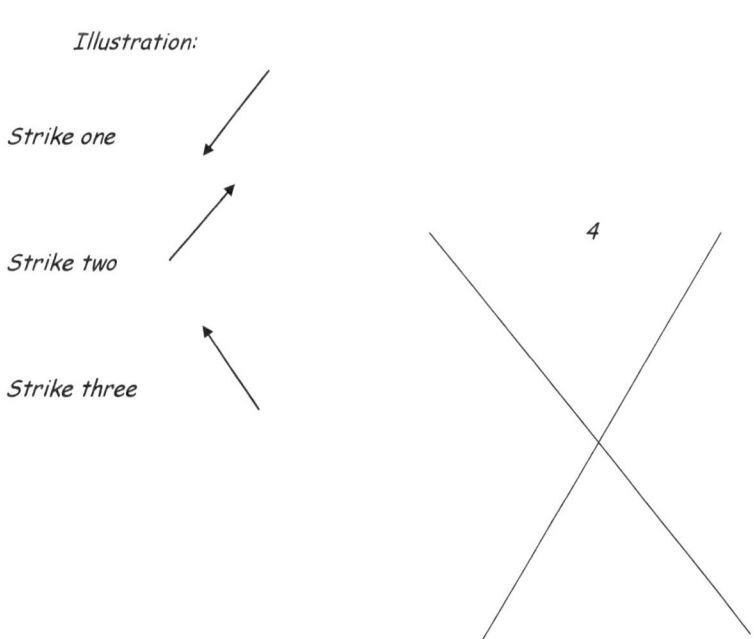

Strike four ↘

                                      6
―――――――――――――――

Strike five ⟵

Strike six ⟶

Technique: 126 345 561 125 435 215 436 653

                1256 2134 5634 3456 4365 6521

Form: 126 345 561 125 435 215 436 653

            1256 2134 5634 3456 4365 6521

Drill: 126 345 561 125 435 215 436 653

            1256 2134 5634 3456 4365 6521

BLOCKING

- Against strike one-

    Technique: From natural stance, raise your weapon hand overhead diagonal pointing downward.

    Form: From natural stance slide your right foot forward and execute the block using your weapon supported by the weak hand.

    Drill: Execute the technique with the feeder attacking the defender.

Illustration:

- Against strike number two (2),

    Technique: From natural stance, lower your weapon hand downward diagonal pointing downward.

Form: From natural stance slide your right foot forward and execute the block using your weapon supported by the weak hand.

Drill: Execute the technique with the feeder attacking the defender.

From upper reinforce block bring it downward and execute low block.

Illustration:

- Against strike three (3)

Technique: From natural stance, raise your weapon hand overhead diagonal pointing downward.

Form: From natural stance slide your right foot forward and execute the block using your weapon supported by the weak hand.

Drill: Execute the technique with the feeder attacking the defender.

Illustration:

- Against strike four (4)-

Technique: From natural stance, raise your weapon hand overhead diagonal pointing downward.

Form: From natural stance slide your right foot forward and execute the block using your weapon supported by the weak hand.

Drill: Execute the technique with the feeder attacking the defender.
From reverse low block bring it to rising block.

Illustration:

- *Against strike five (5)-*
    Technique: *From natural stance, move your weapon hand vertical, pointing downward.*

    Form: *From natural stance slide your right foot forward and execute the block using your weapon supported by the weak hand.*

    Drill: *Execute the technique with the feeder attacking the defender from left foot forward switch to right foot forward and execute outside reinforce block.*

Illustration:

- Against strike Six (6)

Technique: From natural stance, raise your weapon hand vertical pointing downward.

Form: From natural stance slide your lead foot forward and execute the block using your weapon supported by the weak hand.

Drill: Execute the technique with the feeder attacking the defender with the same stances executes inside reinforce block.

Illustration:

COUNTER

1. Against strike number one (1), Technique: From natural stance slide your left foot backward executing the deep forward stance at the same time forehand upward strike hitting your opponent weapon hand and shift your body direction to add the power.

Illustration:

2. Against strike number two (2), from natural stance slide your right foot backward to deep stance, then at the same time launce strike number two hitting your opponent weapon hand.

Illustration:

3. Against strike number three (3), from natural stance slide your right foot backward executing deep stance at the

4. Same time launce strike number four hitting your opponent weapon hand.

Illustration:

5. Against strike number four (4), from natural stance slide your left foot backward executing deep stance at the same time launce strike number five hitting your opponent weapon hand.

Illustration:

6. Against strike number five (5), from natural stance slide your right foot forward then strikes one hitting your opponent weapon hand.

Illustration:

7. Against strike number six (6), from natural stance forward your left foot at the same time launch strike number four hitting your opponent weapon hand.

Illustration:

DOUBLE COUNTER

- *Against strike number one- forehand and back hand slash*

- *Against strike number two – backhand and forehand slash.*

- *Against strike number three – forehand upward and back hand upward.*

- *Against strike number four – back hand downward slash and forehand upward slash.*

- *Against strike number five - forehand upward and back hand downward slash.*

- *Against strike number six – backhand upward and forehand downward slash..*

Single stick Form:

From natural stance, come to feet together to execute bowing, then back to natural stance, slide the lead foot forward and execute a low line vertical downward block then counter with a back hand slash strike then diagonal overhead block with the weak hand support.
Move the back leg about 6 inches to the side as the lead foot follow into a perfect natural fighting stance then deliver a low line attack, move the back leg about 6 inches back as lead foot follow at the same time execute a med section block then assume a checking of opponent weapon hand. Come to feet together or close stance and bow.

Single stick drills:

1. 3 counts
2. 6 counts
3. 6 counts drill moving forward.
4. 6 counts drill moving clockwise
5. 6 counts drill moving counter clockwise

MEDIUM RANGE

Medium Range

This type of fighting range considered to be an intermediate due to the fact that each practitioner knew already the basic fundamentals of the Filipino Martial Arts that involve in the proper use of body mechanics, footwork, stances, and origin of the strikes, proper blockings and body coordination. To make it simple that each combatant with the sticks that measured at least ¾" in diameter and about 29" to 30 inches long can reach the opponents body or to the head, the each practitioner can do some type of drills to develop sensitivity and body coordination.

◄
▲

1. Strikes 1 thru 10 and its corresponding targets. (refer to the diagram)

Striking Patterns for Medium Range Single Stick Single Stick Fighting

The medium range basic sticking pattern is based on a 10 strike system. Ten strikes are easy to remember as you have ten fingers!

Strike #1 is a forehand downward slash /across to the right shoulder/ collar bone.

Strike #2 is a backhand downward slash /across to the left shoulder/collar bone.

Strike #3 is a forehand slash cross the body.

Strike #4 is backhand slash across the body.

Strike #5 is a forehand downward slash cross to the right thigh.

Strike #6 is a backhand downward slash cross to the left thigh.

Strike #7 is a forehand upward slash cross to the right elbow.

Strike #8 is backhand upward slash cross to left elbow.

Strike #9 is a forehand downward slash to the right side of the temple.

Strike #10 is a backhand downward slash to the left side temple.

Technique:

1. 123 214 345 436 567 658 789 8710
2. 125 216 347 478 783 874 9107 1098
3. 1234 2143 3456 4365 5678 6587 78910 87109
4. 12345 21436 34567 43658 56789 658710
5. 123456 214365 345678 436587 5678910 6587109
6. 1234567 2143658 3456789 43658710
7. 12345678 21436587 345678910 436587109
8. 12345678910 21436587109

Form:

All combinations of strikes as refer as numbers will be perform by each practitioner with the combinations of footwork and blockings. Always starts with the natural stance, bowing salutation, back to natural stance, to natural fighting stance then execute the first combination followed by blocking as preparing to step 2. When finished always perform a bowing salutation.

1. 123 214 345 436 567 658 789 8710
2. 125 216 347 478 783 874 9107 1098
3. 1234 2143 3456 4365 5678 6587 78910 87109
4. 12345 21436 34567 43658 56789 658710
5. 123456 214365 345678 436587 5678910 6587109
6. 1234567 2143658 3456789 43658710
7. 12345678 21436587 345678910 436587109
8. 12345678910 21436587109

Drill: This will be performing individually with hitting a fix target or bag.

1. 123 214 345 436 567 658 789 8710
2. 125 216 347 478 783 874 9107 1098
3. 1234 2143 3456 4365 5678 6587 78910 87109
4. 12345 21436 34567 43658 56789 658710
5. 123456 214365 345678 436587 5678910 6587109
6. 1234567 2143658 3456789 43658710
7. 12345678 21436587 345678910 436587109
8. 12345678910 21436587109

Blocks and Blocking

Overview

The ability to block is as important as the ability to hit! Anybody can hit but not everybody can block because they are not trained to. Learn to block quickly and counter strike. First learn to get in the ready position quickly. Stick in the right hand at angle to make one side of the triangle. Left hand (checking hand) ready to check at an angle this makes the other side of the triangle. Your palm edge should be against the stick so you do not get struck by the recoil of your opponent's strike. Your hip's being squared up makes the third. Your stick should never be further than the width of your hand spread away from your body. This allows you to have efficiency in motion a critical concept in the Filipino Martial Art.

- *Blocking on all forehand strike 1, 3, 5, 7, 9*

Starting in the ready position as the defender you slide your strong lead foot to execute a proper fighting stance. Either you are blocking vertical upward or downward position always remember to reinforce your primary block or your weapon with the secondary block which is your weak hand then check your opponents weapon hand.

- Blocking on all the strikes coming from backhand 2,4,6,8,10

Starting from ready position as the defender you slide your strong lead foot to execute a proper fighting stance. Either you are blocking vertical upward or downward position always remember to reinforce your primary block or your weapon with the secondary block which is your weak hand then check your opponents weapon hand.

1. Basic counter against strike 1 thru 10.

Counter Strikes

Counter strikes are done two ways. First is by blocking then counter striking. The second is a parrying block with re-direction. The way I was taught by my Grandpa is just do the reverse of the strike that your opponent is doing. If you are being hit this say with Strike #1 or #2 then use a strike #2 & 1 that's the basic principle but once your familiar with how it works doesn't have to follow the sequence.

Technique

1. Counter strike #1 for strike #1 is strike #2
2. Counter strike #2 for strike #2 is strike #1
3. Counter strike #3 for strike #3 is strike #4
4. Counter strike #4 for strike #4 is strike #3
5. Counter strike #5 for strike #5 is strike #6
6. Counter strike #6 for strike #6 is strike #7
7. Counter strike #7 for strike #7 is strike #8
8. Counter strike #8 for strike #8 is strike #7
9. Counter strike #9 for strike #9 is strike #10
10. Counter strike #10 for strike 10 is strike #9

Form

Form starts with natural stance-bowing- natural stance then execution of the proper stances, blockings, proper breathing and concentration, then back to natural stance – bow.

1. Counter strike #1 for strike #1 is strike #2
2. Counter strike #2 for strike #2 is strike #1
3. Counter strike #3 for strike #3 is strike #4
4. Counter strike #4 for strike #4 is strike #3
5. Counter strike # 5 for strike # 5 is strike #6
6. Counter strike #6 for strike #6 is strike #7
7. Counter strike # 7 for strike # 7 is strike #8
8. Counter strike #8 for strike #8 is strike #7
9. Counter strike #9 for strike # 9 is strike #10
10. Counter strike #10 for strike 10 is strike #9

DRILL

Drills starts with natural stance-bowing- natural stance then execute the following moves with proper execution of stances, blocking, breathing and concentration, then back to natural stance – bow.

- Counter strike #1 for strike #1 is strike #2
- Counter strike #2 for strike #2 is strike #1
- Counter strike #3 for strike #3 is strike #4
- Counter strike #4 for strike #4 is strike #3
- Counter strike # 5 for strike # 5 is strike #6
- Counter strike #6 for strike #6 is strike #7
- Counter strike # 7 for strike # 7 is strike #8
- Counter strike #8 for strike #8 is strike #7
- Counter strike #9 for strike # 9 is strike #10
- Counter strike #10 for strike 10 is strike #9

Technique 1 : Natural stance- slide your lead foot forward as you execute a blocking against a forehand strike using your weapon or stick with your weak hand as a secondary block the slide your weak hand assuming of checking your opponent's weapon hand the back to natural stance.

Technique 1a : Natural stance – slide your weak side foot forward as you execute a blocking against a back hand strike with your weapon and utilize the weak hand as a secondary block then assume a checking of opponent's weapon hand.

Form 1: Bowing salutation – Natural fighting stance as you execute your blocking sequence and continue the other side in reverse position then back to natural stance and bowing.

Drill 1: Two man drill executing the techniques, forms in deferent angles which the other person will be as a feeder and the receiver will demonstrate the whole scenario.

Technique 2:

Natural stance- assume a fighting on guard position and execute a blocking against a forehand high line strike as you use your weak hand to support as a secondary block then assume of checking the opponent's weapon hand. Deliver a backhand counter strike targeting the med section of the body of the attacker then execute a diagonal blocking against a forehand high line strike, again use your weak hand as a secondary block and sensor by checking the attacker's weapon hand.

Form 2:

Bowing salutation - Natural stance- assume a fighting on guard position and execute a blocking against a forehand high line strike as you use your weak hand to support as a secondary block then assume of checking the opponent's weapon hand. Deliver a backhand counter strike targeting the med section of the body of the attacker then execute a diagonal blocking against a forehand high line strike, again use your weak hand as a secondary block and sensor by checking the attacker's weapon hand. Move slide your back foot 6 inches to the right side as your lead foot follow and deliver a counter forehand strike to the med section of opponent's body, then assume a vertical block against mid section attack and assume palm up as you're catching the opponent's weapon hand then deliver a forehand high line strike. Bowing salutation.

DRILL 2:

1. *2 counts drill*
2. *3 counts drill*
3. *6 counts drill*
4. *6 counts drill in straight line back and forth.*
5. *6 counts drill moving clockwise*
6. *6 counts drill moving counter-clockwise*

DISARMING

In the application of basic disarming you should emphasize the proper application of blocking, checking to either holds and kaw-it. The technique of wresting away or seizing the weapon from the opponent is another important aspect of arnis. Generally known as agaw, or pangilog in some regions of the country, the technique can be performed by the empty hand, the olisi, or a combination of the two. In the past, a good eskrimador (practitioner of eskrima) was often measured by his ability to disarm an opponent with finesse and exceptional proficiency. Through the years, continually search for creative ways to express the fundamental principles of these techniques. The very basic disarming is what we called the snake disarm, this was the progression of skills after learning how to block the will be followed by a disarm known as sneak disarming.

Disarming against forehand strike, the defender should be in proper balance of footwork, then block the incoming strike with your sticks or weapon followed by a secondary block or the weak hand then slide the weak hand to opponents weapon hand under forearm going upward pointing the sky at the same time twisting your body to opposite direction followed with a push using your forearm to complete the disarm.

Disarming against backhand strike, the defender should be in proper balance of footwork then block the incoming strike with your weapon or stick followed by secondary block then checking the opponents weapon hand then slide your stick underneath pointing the sky followed by pushing your opponents weapon hand downward to complete the disarm.

Technique 1:
Natural stance - Slide your lead foot forward into a fighting forward stance as you execute vertical blocking, use the weak hand as secondary block. Your weak hand will slide to reach opponent's weapon hand and go under it as you point your fingers upward and use your weapon forearm to assist your weak hand to take away the weapon.

Technique 1a:
Slide your weak side foot forward into a fighting reverse forward stance as you execute vertical blocking, use the weak hand as secondary block. Your weapon hand will slide to reach opponent's weapon hand forearm and you scope under your opponent's weapon hand pointing your weapon vertical upward and assume of pushing your opponent's weapon hand with your weak hand to take away the weapon.

FORM 1:
Bowing salutation- Natural stance – Slide your lead foot forward into a fighting forward stance as you execute vertical blocking, use the weak hand as secondary block. Your weak hand will slide to reach opponent's weapon hand and go under it, as you point your fingers upward and use your weapon forearm to assist your weak hand to take away the weapon. Back to natural stance the bow.

FORM 1a:
Bowing salutation- Slide your weak side foot forward as you execute vertical blocking, use the weak hand as secondary block. Your weak hand will slide to reach opponent's weapon hand and you scope under your opponent's weapon hand pointing upward and push your opponent's weapon hand with your weak hand to take away the weapon.

DRILL 1:

1. *Disarm against forehand strike (high line attack)*
2. *Disarm against forehand strike (mid section)*
3. *Disarm against forehand strike(low line attack)*
4. *Disarm against backhand strike (high line attack)*
5. *Disarm against backhand strike (mid section attack)*
6. *Disarm against backhand strike (low line attack)*

Close Range

When each fighter get to closed that their body is in contact with each other, and all that they learned in previous segment regarding sensitivity will apply into some kind of trapping opponents weapon hand and defection in order to apply the short range strikes that includes: flick strikes, vertical jabs, horizontal jabs and twirls.

Note: These three ranges of fighting in Filipino Martial Arts could be interchange in the applications depending in each practitioner.

5. Kinds of strikes

   1. Slashing strike: it can be vertical or horizontal, but this type of strikes is either came from forehand and backhand. To make sure that you are doing it right, think that your holding a sword or any bladed weapons and when you swing you should always think of hitting first with the blade or you couldn't cut. This type of strikes is very effective in both long range and medium especially if you use your body torque.

   2. Circular strikes can be vertical and horizontal motion but it came from forehand or backhand. Most vulnerable target is head, trunk, shoulders and weapon hand.

   3. Curbing strikes is by snapping you from palm up position to downward position (Forehand) and from palm down position to palm up position (Backhand) and you can hit your intended target either high and low. Most of the time the vulnerable target will be the back side of the body and the head.

4. Flick or a jab could be high and low depending in your intended target. Most of the time the vulnerable target will be the head and weapon hand.

SHORT RANGE COMMON STRIKES

1. Twirl (vertical downward/upward, diagonal forehand /backhand)
2. Curb (forehand low/high, backhand low/high)
3. Flick (forehand and backhand low and forehand and backhand high)

Striking combinations in short range.

1. 2 combo - forehand flick high/forehand downward twirl
2. 2 combo -backhand high flick/ backhand downward twirl
3. 2 combo- flick/twirl forehand (low)
4. 2 combo- flick/twirl backhand (high)
5. 3 combo - forehand flick high/forehand downward twirl/backhand curve to the body.
6. 3 combo- backhand flick high/backhand downward twirl/forehand curve to the body.
7. 3 combo- high forehand and backhand flick to the head and forehand twirl.
8. 3 combo - high backhand /forehand flick to the head and a backhand downward twirl.
9. 3 combo- forehand curve to the body/head follow by forehand twirl
10. 3 combo - backhand curve to the body and head follow by a backhand twirl.

TECHNIQUE 1 : Natural stance- Slide your lead foot forward assume an on guard or fighting stance position, extend your weak hand as catching the opponent's incoming forehand strike with your open palm then close the gap between the body, then execute a forehand butt of your stick or weapon aiming the collar none or cubicle of your opponent.

TECHNIQUE 1a : Natural stance- Slide your lead foot forward assume an on guard or fighting stance position, extend your weak hand assuming a parry or following the force of the opponent's incoming forehand strike with your open palm then close the gap between the body, then execute a forehand butt of your stick or weapon aiming the collar none or cubicle of your opponent.

TECHNIQUE 1 b: Natural stance- Slide your lead foot forward assume an on guard or fighting stance position, extend your weak hand assuming catch and parry or following the force of the opponent's incoming forehand strike with your open palm then close the gap between the body, then execute a forehand butt of your stick or weapon aiming the collar none or cubicle of your opponent.

TECHNIQUE 1c: Natural stance- Slide your lead foot forward assume an on guard or fighting stance position, extend your weak hand as catching the opponent's incoming forehand strike with your open palm then close the gap between the body, then check opponents weapon hand with your weapon hand forearm as you assume open palm up catching opponent's arm then execute a forehand butt of your stick or weapon aiming the collar none or cubicle of your opponent.

TECHNIQUE 1d: Natural stance- Slide your lead foot forward assume an on guard or fighting stance position, extend your weak hand assuming a parry or following the force of the opponent's incoming forehand strike with your open palm then close the gap between the body, then check opponent's weapon hand with your weapon forearm. Execute a forehand butt of your stick or weapon aiming the collar none or cubicle of your opponent.

FORM 1:

Bowing salutation- Natural stance- Slide your lead foot forward assume an on guard or fighting stance position, extend your weak hand as catching the opponent's incoming forehand strike with your open palm then close the gap between the body, then execute a forehand butt of your stick or weapon aiming the collar none or cubicle of your opponent. Back to natural stance then bow.

FORM 1a:

Bowing salutation - Natural stance- Slide your lead foot forward assume an on guard or fighting stance position, extend your weak hand assuming a parry or following the force of the opponent's incoming forehand strike with your open palm then close the gap between the body, then execute a forehand butt of your stick or weapon aiming the collar none or cubicle of your opponent. Back to natural stance then bow.

FORM 1b:

Bowing salutation - Natural stance- Slide your lead foot forward assume an on guard or fighting stance position, extend your weak hand assuming catch and parry or following the force of the opponent's incoming forehand strike with your open palm then close the gap between the body, then execute a forehand butt of your stick or weapon aiming the collar none or cubicle of your opponent. Back to natural stance then bow.

FORM 1c:
Bowing salutation - Natural stance- Slide your lead foot forward assume an on guard or fighting stance position, extend your weak hand as catching the opponent's incoming forehand strike with your open palm then close the gap between the body, then check opponents weapon hand with your weapon hand forearm as you assume open palm up catching opponent's arm then execute a forehand butt of your stick or weapon aiming the collar none or cubicle of your opponent. Back to natural stance the bow.

FORM 1d:
Bowing salutation - Natural stance- Slide your lead foot forward assume an on guard or fighting stance position, extend your weak hand assuming a parry or following the force of the opponent's incoming forehand strike with your open palm then close the gap between the body, then check opponent's weapon hand with your weapon forearm. Execute a forehand butt of your stick or weapon aiming the collar none or cubicle of your opponent. Back to natural stance then bow.

DRILL

1. Catching opponent's incoming forehand strike
2. Parrying opponent's incoming back hand strike
3. Catching and parrying opponent's incoming forehand srike
4. Catching with your weak hand the opponent's incoming forehand strike then check with your forearm and catch opponent's weapon hand forearm with your palm up the incoming low line attack.
5, Parrying opponent's incoming forehand strike, check with your weapon's hand forearm and catch the opponent's weapon arm as you trap opponent's weapon arm.

TECHNIQUE 2: Natural stance - Slide your lead foot forward assume an on guard or fighting stance position, extend your weak hand as catching the opponent's incoming forehand strike with your open palm then close the gap between the body, then check opponents weapon hand with your weapon hand forearm as you deliver a direct backhand strike to opponents head.

FORM 2: Bowing salutation - Natural stance- Slide your lead foot forward assume an on guard or fighting stance position, extend your weak hand as catching the opponent's incoming forehand strike with your open palm then close the gap between the body, then check opponents weapon hand with your weapon hand forearm, as you deliver a direct backhand strike to opponents head. Back to natural stance then bow.

DRILL2:

    1. 2 counts- Natural fighting position, block the incoming strike with your weak hand open palm, check opponents weapon hand with your weapon hand forearm as you deliver a backhand strike to the right temple of your opponent.

TECHNIQUE 3: Natural stance - Slide your lead foot forward assume an on guard or fighting stance position, extend your weak hand as catching the opponent's incoming forehand strike with your open palm then close the gap between the body, then check opponents weapon hand with your weapon hand forearm as you deliver a direct backhand strike and forehand strike / hit to opponents head.

FORM 3: Bowing salutation - Natural stance- Slide your lead foot forward assume an on guard or fighting stance position, extend your weak hand as catching the opponent's incoming forehand strike with your open palm then close the gap between the body, then check opponents weapon hand with your weapon hand forearm, as you deliver a direct backhand strike and forehand strike / hit to opponents head. Back to natural stance then bow.

DRILL 3:

    1. 3 counts- Natural fighting position, block the incoming strike with your weak hand open palm, check opponents weapon hand with your weapon hand forearm as you deliver a backhand/forehand strike to the head of your opponent.

TECHNIQUE4:

Natural stance - Slide your lead foot forward assume an on guard or fighting stance position, extend your weak hand as catching the opponent's incoming forehand strike with your open palm then close the gap between the body, then check opponents weapon hand with your weapon hand forearm as you deliver a direct backhand strike and forehand strike / hit to opponents head and a backhand slash cross opponent's body.

FORM 4:

Bowing salutation - Natural stance- Slide your lead foot forward assume an on guard or fighting stance position, extend your weak hand as catching the opponent's incoming forehand strike with your open palm then close the gap between the body, then check opponents weapon hand with your weapon hand forearm, as you deliver a direct backhand strike and forehand strike / hit to opponents head and a backhand slash strike cross opponents body. Back to natural stance then bow.

DRILL 4:

1. 4 counts- Natural fighting position, block the incoming strike with your weak hand open palm, check opponents weapon hand with your weapon hand forearm as you deliver a backhand/forehand strike to the head and a backhand slash cross opponent's body.

TECHNIQUE 5:

Natural stance- Slide your lead foot forward assume an on guard or fighting stance position, extend your weak hand assuming catch and parry or following the force of the opponent's incoming forehand strike with your open palm down, Deliver a forehand and backhand strike to opponent's head at the same time changing the position of your open palm up, then finish it with a forehand slash strike cross opponents body.

FORM 5:

Bowing- Natural stance- Slide your lead foot forward assume an on guard or fighting stance position, extend your weak hand assuming catch and parry or following the force of the opponent's incoming forehand strike with your open palm down, Deliver a forehand and backhand strike to opponent's head at the same time changing the position of your open palm up, then finish it with a forehand slash strike cross opponents body. Back to natural stance then bow.

DRILL 5:

1. 4 counts - Natural stance- Slide your lead foot forward assume an on guard or fighting stance position, parry or following the force of the opponent's incoming forehand strike with your open palm down position, Deliver a forehand and backhand strike to opponent's head at the same time changing the position of your open palm up, then finish it with a forehand slash strike cross opponents body. Back to natural stance then bow.

AUTHORS PROFILE

Current

- *Filipino Martial Arts Grand Master*
- *CEO of ROILES GEAR Ltd. the leading manufacturer of Filipino Martial Arts Product / equipment*
- *Martial Arts Instructional Film Producer*
- *Founder of PAKAMUT International Association*

Education/Training High School- College Cebu State of Science and Technology, Cebu Philippines

1984-1985 Cebu Technical School, Cebu, Philippines

2006- Criminal Justice, Stratford University

1985 - 1987 Philippine National Police Training Officer PC / INP Training Center, Lahug, Cebu City, Philippines

2001- Firearms Training, Defensive Tactics, Handcuffing, Counter Terrorism Bomb Treats Procedures, Law, Crimes Offenses and Arrest Authority, Cardiopulmonary, Resuscitation, First Aid, Preventing Disease Transmission and PR-24 Quest Intelligence Bureau, Ltd. Las Vegas NV, U.S.A.

2006- Peace Officer Standard Training - PC832 Module 1,2,3 Rio Hondo College Whittier CA.

2006- Criminal Justice - Stratford University

2006- Fire Arms Instructor Course NATIONAL RIFLE ASSOCIATION (NRA)U.S.A.

Certified Pistol Instructor, State of California and NRA

Felix Roiles Summary

FELIX ROILES -- Filipino Martial Arts Grand Master, Martial Arts Seminar Presenter, Speaker, Fire Arms instructor.

I welcome all invitations to connect! (Open Net worker)
Connect with me @ Email: flxroiles@yahoo.com

A FEW QUICK FACTS ABOUT ME:

♦ Founder of PAKAMUT International

♦ Hand to Hand Combat, Fire Arms and Edged Weapons Expert

♦ 30 Years experience in training top level Law Enforcement, Military, and Security Personnel

♦ Personal Security Consultant for Celebrities, Politicians, Executives, and family members of High-Profile Individuals

♦ Motivational Speaker and presenter for Martial Artists, Corporations, Private Interests & Charities

♦ Conducted hundreds of Martial Arts Training Seminars worldwide

♦ Martial Arts Instructional Film Producer and Fight Choreographer

♦ Martial Arts Product Researcher, Developer and Consultant (Protective Gear Lines, Training Weapons, Instructional DVDs)

Specialties

Filipino Martial Arts Grand Master, Martial Arts Seminar Presenter, Speaker, Executive Security Consultant, Filipino Martial Arts, Certified Fire Arms Instructor, Motivational Speaker, Law Enforcement, Military, Security Personnel, Martial Arts Instructional Film Producer, Martial Arts Product Researcher, Developer and Consultant, International Martial Arts Training Seminars, Martial Artist, Personal Security, Consultant, Celebrities, Politicians, Executives, CEOs and their families

Felix Roiles's Experience

Martial Arts Consultant ♦ Filipino Martial Arts Sports Product Development

Sporting Goods industry
1992 – Present
Stick Fighting and Blade Sport tournament for international competition.

Manufacturer of Filipino Martial Arts equipment for training, tournament and sparring, being sold worldwide

Martial Arts Instructional Film Producer ♦ Founder & CEO ValFlex Production

Professional Training

I have produced and appeared in Martial Arts Instructional Films & Videos that are now being sold in over 80 countries.

Martial Arts Grand Master ♦ CEO ♦ Founder ♦ Personal Security Consultant
Worldwide Martial Arts organization dedicated to the preservation and promotion of all Filipino Martial Arts

Tactical training for military, law enforcement, executives, celebrities, private studios, and experienced martial artists.

Personal security. Consultant for high-profile individuals and their families.

Martial Arts Seminar Presenter ♦

Books and Magazine: Featured Inside Kung Fu Magazine May 2008 issue, PAKAMUT Special Edition of FMA digest, California Examiner, World Reporter, Sunstar Daily, Freeman, Taliba, Orange County Reporter, Philippine Daily News, World Escrima, Kali Arnis (WEKAF) 2004 issue, WEKAF 1996 issue, PAKAMUT BOOK AUTHOR- the Filipino Fighting Arts System, Eskrima Kali Arnis Book by GM Dionisio Canete. MARTIAL ARTS HISTORY MUSEUM BOOK.

Video: Starring/ Produce in Doce Pares Muli-Style Instructional Video Volume 1,2, AND 3

Training Background: 35 years of Filipino Fighting Arts System teaching/ Training. (FILIPINO MARTIAL ART)

Instructors:

- *Grand Master Andes "BAGARI" Roiles(PAKAMUT) 1969-1986*
- *Grand Master Benidicto Roiles (PAKAMUT) 1969-1996*
- *Master Jacinto Sarvida 1982-1993 Combat Judo Karate Fed Phil.(COJUKAF)*
- *Professor Julio Villaflores- Phil. YAW-YAN.1981-1986*
- *Grand Master Auring Lasola of OLIBAMA ESKRIMA. 1987*
- *Master Poring Siroy the BLADE MASTER of Ihawan Mandaue city. 1998*
- *Sensei Jesus Flores of Black Eagle Martial Art 1984-1993*
- *Master Punyong Oro the Bugno Master 1972-1980*
- *Master Ito Ubayan.1972-1980*
- *Master Constantino " LAPU-LAPU" Loy-loy.1973-1980*
- *Sensei Roger Requillo KUNTAW ng PILIPINAS. 1988-1990*
- *Grand Master Dionisio " Diony" Canete DOCE PARES 1992-1996*
- *Sensei Willy Aloba of DO-KYOHAN Karate. 1981-1992*

SPECIAL SKILLS:

- Physical Security Specialist
- Martial Art / Self-defense Expert.
- Handgun/Pistol Certified Instructor

MARTIAL ART STYLES:
- PAKAMUT /fma
- Doce Pares Multi-Style System
- Freestyle Eskrima Kali-Arnis
- Combat Judo Karate
- Kickboxing

EXPOSEURE:

- Conduct Training/ assistance to U.S. Marine Special Operation Command held at Camp Dawson, West Virginia, U.S.A. 2006

- Conduct demo/presentation during the Philippine American Expo in Los Angeles Convention Center, Los Angeles, CA. August 16, 2002.

- Conduct demonstration during the Philippine American Exposition August 14, 2003 in Fairgrounds Del Mar San Diego, California.

- Conduct demo for Martial Art for Christ in Sta. Ana California, August 2003.

- Coach/ Trainer of Roiles Freestyle Martial Arts team and Champion Trophy for most winners in a team for 1st Annual Doce Pares International Full Contact Stick Fighting Tournament on 9th of May in Cerritos, CA. 1998

- *Coach/ Trainer of Martial Arts team for Northern California Eskrima Kali-Arnis Federation (NCEKAF) Tournament of Champions on 6th of December in Sacramento CA. in 1997.*

- *Coached/Trainer Philippines team delegation for the 4th World Eskrima Kali-Arnis Championship tournament on June 7-9 Carson, CA U.S.A.*

- *Conducted FMA Training seminars in Kope City, Yamashi Ken, Japan 1993*

- *Conducted Training for Revirine Seaborne Special Action Team of Philippines Army and Philippine National police Senior Officers (defensive tactics)*

- *Conducted a series demonstration in Phil cite Center in Cebu, Philippines in 1991.*

HONORS:

- *Martial Art Masters Hall of Fame*

- *Grand MASTER (Filipino Martial Art)*

- *Founder/Director-Thumb cat Freestyle Martial art Eskrima Kali-Arnis. (Philippines)*

- *CHAMPION Doce Pares Annual World Congress and Championship, Circus-Circus Hotel / Casino, Las Vegas NV. U. S. A. 2003*

- *Over all Champion – Battle of Carson Full Contact Stick Fighting Championship June 12, 2004. Carson California.*

- *Award of Recognition during BLACK BELT SPECTACULAR 2003.*

- *Award of Appreciation for dedication to martial Arts given by KADAN Martial Arts on 29th of March in Long Beach CA. in 1998.*

- ***WORLD CHAMPION*****:** *2nd World Eskrima Kali Arnis World Championship 1992 Manila Philippines.*

- *M.V.P. Award during the 2nd World Eskrima Kali Arnis Federation Championship 1992 Manila Philippines*

- *WORLDCHAMPION: 3rd World Eskrima Kali Arnis (WEKAF) Championship 1994 Quezon City, Philippines.*

- *Special Award- Northern California Eskrima Kali-Arnis Federation (WEKAF) 6th of December 1998- Sacramento CA.*

- *Special Awards- (WEKAF) Western Regional Championships on 4th of October 1997 Oakland, CA U.S.A.*

- *WORLD CHAMPION - World Eskrima Kali-Arnis championships and Congress April 2003, Circus-Circus Hotel Casino, Las Vegas Nevada.*

- *Award of recognition at 11th Cebu All Sports awards in March 27 1993.*

- *Undefeated - Full Contact Stick Fighting Champion for Quest for the Best Eskrima Kali Arnis tournaments in the Philippines. 1990-1996*

- *Special Award of extra ordinary Achievement- February 10 in Catmon Cebu, Philippines.*

- *Sports Award - 10th Cebu All Sports Award in March.*

- *National Champion – Karate-do- Southern Philippines Open Karate-do tournament on August 4, Davao City Philippines in 1991.*

- *Silver medal- Congressional Cup Duel of International Karate Champions on April 15 in Metro Manila Philippines.*

- *Regional Karate Champion- Visayas and Mindanao Regional Karate tournament on June 16 in Sundowner Center Point in Cebu, Philippines in 1993.*

- *Champion- Best of the Best Blood sport Part II at ICC gym in Ozamis City, Philippines.*

- *Regional Karate Champion-Visayas and Mindanao Regional Karate Tournament on March 11 in Cebu YMCA Philippines 1990.*

- *National Karate Champion- National Open Karate Tournament on June 19 in Davao City Philippines in 1988.*

- *Champion- Battle of Karate Champions at the University of Visayas in Cebu Philippines.*

- *Champion 1st Invitational Karate Tournament in Billaba Lyte, Philippines 1985.*

- *Karate Champion- 1997 Battle of Champions Open weight division in Lapu-Lapu City Philippines in 1987.*

- *5 times undefeated Karate Team Champion Visayas and Mindanao Region.*

- *Champion- YAW-YAN Full Contact KickBoxing Championship, Mandaue City, September1985 in Madaue, City Cebu Philippines.*

- *Champion- Competition-2nd Black Belt Open Invitational Battle of Karate Team Championships on October 21, 1983 Metro Cebu, Philippines.*

- *Second place - Philippines Shotokan 1st Open Karate-do tournament August 5, 182 in Naga, Cebu, Philippines*

- *Champion- Lightweight Regional Meet Boxing Association of vocational Institution of the Philippines (AVIP) in 1980.*

MEMBERSHIPS:

- *PAKAMUT INTERNATIONAL ASSOC.*
- *National Rifle Association (U.S.A.)*
- *ROILES FREESTYLE Martial Art (Philippines)*
- *World Eskrima Kali-Arnis Federation (WEKAF).*
- *United State Filipino Martial Art (USFMA)*
- *National Arnis Eskrima Kali Association of the Philippines (NARAPHIL)*
- *DOCE PARES International.*
- *Congress of American Knife Fighters. (U.S.A.)*
- *Combat Judo Karate Federation of the Philippines (COJUKAF).*
- *World Union Karate-do Organization (WUKO)*
- *Philippine Karate-do Federation (PKF)*
- *Central Visayas Karate Association (CVKA)*
- *Cebu Lion Karate Club.*
- *Lincoln Self-defense Karate club (LSDKC)*

ACHIEVEMENTS:

- 2010 Martial Art Masters Hall of Fame

- 2006 Special Award Given by Los Angeles City Council
- Hosted 2nd Annual Los Angeles Open Full Contact Stick Fighting Championship Los Angeles, CA U.S.A.
- Hosted 1st Annual Los Angeles Open Full Contact Stick Fighting Championship, December 11, 2005. Los Angeles CA.
- Over all Champion Battle of Carson Full Contact Stick Fighting Championship Carson, CA. June 12, 2004.
- Special Award of Recognition as World Champion/ community leader during the
  Philippine American Expo August 16, 2003. Fairground   Del Mar, San Diego, CA.
- Special Award of recognition in City of Carson, CA 1998
- April 2003: Produce Instructional video for the Filipino Martial Art (Doce Pares Multi style System) series 1,2 and 3
- 2002: Special Award of recognition Black Belt Spectacular, Cypress College, California, U.S.A.
- 2003: Special Award of Martial Arts (KADAN martial arts) Garden Grove, CA. U.S.A.
- January 2003 Established Flex Services Inc. / ValFlex Production Inc.
- April 2003: Champion of 1st Doce Pares World Championship and Congress in circus-circus Hotel and casino Las Vegas NV. U.S.A.

For more information please visit: www.google.com/master felix roiles, www.youtube/pakamut www.expedia.com/master felix roiles. www.roilesgear.com

Footage

Pakamut Int'l Assoc. Team headed by Grand Master Felix Roiles won over all championship trophies during Battle of Carson Eskrima Kali Arnis Championship held on June 12, 2004. From L-R Romeo Santos, Alan Santos, Pat Fletch, Arnold Santos, Edgar Banzon, Felix Roiles, Tim Natlie. Sitting L-R Elvis Tabongar, Robert Kincaid and Sonny Sanico.

Grand Master Felix Roiles and Master Erwin Mosqueda during a demo for Martial Art for Christ in Santa Ana California held on October 2004.

Alan Santos and Grand Master Felix Roiles doing knife demonstration.

Martial Art History Museum 2004

Grand Master Felix Roiles, Howard Jackson, and Rafael Koche

With Alec Baldwin   with Sifu R. Bustillo   Hector Camacho (movie Producer)

James Lew   Bong Yu, Bob Wall & F   R. Koche&
Bill

Helpful words

Visayan	Tagalog	English
Abtik	Mabilis	Quick
Ako	Ako	Me
Agwanta	Tiis	Patience
Amahan	Tatay	Father
Anak	Anak	Son/Daughter
Andam	Handa	Ready
Anhi	Lapit	Come
Asa	Saan	Where
Ayaw	Huwag	Don't
Badlis	Linya	Line
Bag-o	Bago	New
Bati	Pangit	Ugly
Boutan	Mabait	Kind
Bunal	Yantok	Sticks
Dagan	Takbo	Run
Dali	Bilis	Hurry
Daku	Malaki	Big
Dili	Hindi	No
Dunggab	Sak-sak	Trush
Gahi	**Tigas**	**Hard**
Gahig Ulo	**Matigas and ulo**	**hard headed**
Gahom	**Kapangyarihan**	**Power**
Gawas	Labas	Outside
Gibati	pakiramdam	feelings
Gunit	Hawak	Hold
Hadlok	Takot	Scared
Hapak	Sapak	Hit
Hayag	Liwanag	Light
Hinay	Mahina	Slow
Husay	Ayusin	Settle

Igsoon	Kapatid	Brother
Ilado	Kilala	Famous
Isog	Matapang	Tough
Kaaway	Kalaban	Enemy
Kamot	Kamay	Hand
Kauban	Kasama	Buddy
Kinsa	Sino	Who
Kumo	Kamao	Fist
Kusog	Lakas	Strenght
Labay	Tapon	Throw
Layo	**Malayo**	**Far**
Lihok	Galaw	Move
Lingkod	Upo	Set
Lubag	Baluktutin	Twist
Lukso	Talon	Jump
Luya	Pagod	Tired
Maayo	Mabuti	Good
Maayong Buntag	Magandang Umaga	Good Morning
Maayong Gabi-e	Magandang Gabi	Good Evening
Maayong Hapon	Magandang Hapon	Good Afternoon
Malipayon	Masaya	Happy
Mangtutudlo	Guro	Teacher/Instructor
Nakadaog	Panalo	Winner
Napildi	Natalo	Lost
Ngano	Bakit	Why
O	Oo	Yes
Padayun	Tuloy	Continue
Paminaw	Makinig	Listen
Panalipod	Pagtanggol	Depend
Pangu	Pangulo	Chief
Patid	Sipa	Kick
Pikas	Kabila	Otherside
Sagpa	Sampal	Slap
Sakop	Pangkat	Group
Sugo	Utos	Command
Sugod	Umpisa	Start
Sulod	Loob	Inside
Sulti	Sabi	Tell

Sumbag	Suntok	Punch
Taas	Itaas	Above
Talawan	Takot	Coward
Tapulan	**Tamad**	**Lazy**
Tigulang	Matanda	Old
Tikasan	Mandaraya	Cheater
Tindog	Tayu	Stand
Tuman	Sang ayon	Follow
Tumba	Bagsak	Fall
Tuo	Kanan	Right
Tuyok	Ikot	Twirl
Ubos	Baba	Below
Undang	Hinto	Quit
Unsa	Ano	What
Uyuan	Tiyohin	Uncle
Wa'la	Kaliwa	Left
Yukbo	Yuko	Bow

NUMBERS

Ihap	Bilang	Counting
Usa	Isa	One
Duha	Dalawa	Two
Tulo	Tatlo	Three
Upat	Apat	Four
Lima	Lima	Five
Unom	Anim	Six
Pito	Pito	Seven
Walo	Walo	Eight
Siyam	Siyam	Nine
Napulo	**Sampu**	**Ten**

My name is Felix Roiles born on Oct 20, 1965 in Bongyas Catmon Cebu, Philippines. I came here in the United States of America on June 6, 1996 as delegate from the Philippines for the 4th World Eskrima Kali Arnis World Championship in United State June 6, 1996. After the competition I decided to staying in the US for better future of my family that I left behind in the Philippines. When I came in this country I only have few dollars in my pocket, determination, skills that I learned from my humble Grand Father and courage to achieved of what's in my mind , which is a change and for a better future of my family, relatives and for Filipino people. Now a days thinking of what I been thru in my life I decided to write something about how it started and how my dreams became a reality.

I was born and raised in barangay Bongyas, town Catmon, province Cebu, Philippines. Town of Catmon is more than 100 mile away from the populous area of Cebu city and barangay Bonyas is a mountainous barangay of Catmon more or less 20 miles from the town which is located and boundary of neighboring town of north, south, east and western towns of Cebu. My parent were farmers who couldn't afford to send their children to school, the way we live, we don't have anything that the new generations have, we are very self reliance that we defend on what the nature have. We only come to the town market once a moth to get some salt or to sell some of our farm products, which nobody wants to go because it will take at least 5-6 hours walking by foot carrying the produce in your back to sell in the market.

When I was growing as kid we don't have any kind of toys that other kids have what we have is a piece of stick that we called a poor man's toy that you can do a lot of different use and its fun. My grand father Andres Roiles was the one everybody look up because he was so well respected in our barangay, great as a family man but also his skills in fighting that he impart to his family as a treasure to our generation.

Our families always gather in the afternoon after the works in the farm kind of socializing and honing the skills in fighting, because with out the skills you won't be a good person because you can't stand by your self and defend your family according to grandpa. So it was kind of mandatory besides it is fun that even after the regular work out me and my brothers still do it till dark the resume when the moon shine at night.

When my grandpa begun to train me, aside from the regular session that we had in the family, he told me of how he learned it from talking about the great ancestor that handed the skills to his family, and what my responsibilities, values are and when to use the knowledge that I'm going to have. He told me to pull out my pinuti blade and he said to cut the banana bunch, and later on he explained to me that in the real fight three major parts of the human body that are very effective target to finish the fight right away. He showed me how to swing it right in forehand targeting the neck and horizontal backhand strike targeting the body and a forehand strike targeting the leg, and the use of proper foot works and body mechanics. All those things that he taught me became part of me and help me to overcome all the obstacles and boulders that I've been through in life.

Kind of funny when me and my brother Alex sat down in a big rocks in the mountain overlooking the ocean back in the days when I was young before I started going to primary school, one day since we don't have a clock or no one in the family own one, we knew that its 12:00 noon when an airplane passed by the sky and it's time to call the family members working in the farm that it is lunch time, in a quick moment I told my brother that one day I'm going to ride that airplane to see my grandpas brother Eugenio in America who is a great hero in the family and my brother laughing out loud and told my parents when we got back to the house that I became crazy because of what I said, they were laughing except my mom and my dad who steered at me and what

I thought both of them became sad, I also become guilty of what I said, I don't mean to hurt them, I love them so much. Many years came by setting on the same spot that me and my brother hangout when I saw a tiny moving vessels that we can see in a very far away I asked my brother please don't tell our parents what I tell you...and my brother said okay.... I told him that someday I will go far away from home and my brother became very sad and asked me why? I told him I want to see beyond that horizon.

What I learned from my humble grandpa brought me of where I'm at right now and realized when I got in the United State of how valuable the lessons that he taught me and the treasure from our family as part of the Filipino culture.

I was kind of hesitant not to shared my story and just keep it myself, but I also realized how important the culture where I came from and how proud I am of where I came from.

Grandpa said "Skill, courage and positive thinking are the key for survival"... . "KISS.....Keep It Super Simple". "DOT... Direct On Target"

GM Felix Roiles

The PAKAMUT fighting system, as taught by GM Felix Roiles, was handed down to him by his humble grandfather, a true Master in the Filipino Fighting Arts. Using a very simple method, this art utilizes the body's natural movements in highly effective forms of fighting techniques with the use of impact & edged weapons, and hand-to-hand combat. PAKAMUT in Cebuano means the 'Pilipino Fighting System and Style'. It was believed that Datu Mangal, the father of Datu Lapu-lapu, was the first Pilipino hero to bring the art of fighting to the island. Datu Mangal was a direct descendant of the leaders of the powerful Sri - Visayan Empire of 13th century Malay, who conquered and colonized many lands. After the empire was taken over by the Maja Pahit Empire of ancient Sumatra and Borneo, the 10 Datu and their kinsmen settled on the island of Visayan where the art continued to be refined into what we see today.

About the Author

Grand Master Felix Roiles is a two-time World Full Contact Stick Fighting Champion, and is the recipient of numerous awards in various martial art disciplines. Since childhood, he has spent his life in training in the martial arts and is a descendant of Datu Lapu-lapu. This text is a result of his desires to teach the ancient Cebuano fighting style that he learned from his humble grandfather, Andres Roiles, who raised him in the remote mountain area of Catmon, Cebu, Philippines. In 1983, he started "PAKAMUT", in honor of that art. He has won every major tournament in local and national competition in full contact stick fighting (hosted by NARAPHIL) and the World Eskrima Kali Arnis Federation (WEKAF). He was a member of the Doce Pares 'Elite Team' lead by Master Percival " Val " Pableo and successfully dominated the 2nd World Eskrima Kali Arnis Championship. The team defeated the rivals in 21 countries and is considered by many to be the stickfighters ever assembled. Today, GM Roiles lives in Southern California and actively trains students around the world.

#BO2001A

Carson, CA 90745
www.iiSports.com

$29.95

www.ingramcontent.com/pod-product-compliance
Lightning Source LLC
Chambersburg PA
CBHW070946230426

43666CB00011B/2584